GROWING UP ITALIAN IN THE 50's

Or How Most of Us Became Good Wise Guys

THOMAS DEPAOLI

A Growing Up Memories Book

ISBN: 1467992364
ISBN-13: 9781467992367

Library of Congress control Number: 2011962405
CreateSpace, North Charleston, South Carolina

Contents

Introduction

I enjoyed growing up in the fifties! This book shares a few of the stories about my youth and our family traditions. Although we had Italian customs that my parents, aunts, and uncles valued, they greatly wanted us to become Americanized. I wrote this book to capture the experiences of growing up and how that era seemed to be more supportive and nurturing for children. These experiences were too much fun to be lost and forgotten. Not every one of us turned out the better from this upbringing, but most of us did. To feel nostalgic and believe that way of life can be captured again is unrealistic; however, many of the positive aspects can serve as lessons today.

Some of the stories are humorous, some are factual, and others capture the person or event. I wrote them to preserve the memories and to honor my relatives who are no longer with us. The stories are not meant to be great works of literature, rather my personal reminiscences. Many readers, because they are not family, may not enjoy the lessons of these stories. I urge them to be patient and just find the ones that bring back their own good memories.

I was definitely a "challenge" growing up. I was rambunctious, inquisitive, and prone to try anything for fun. Luckily I had a lot of relatives making sure I didn't get into serious trouble. I am forever grateful to them.

In the fifties, everyone seemed to care about us as children and participated in raising us. There was no hesitation on the part of my aunts or uncles to correct and guide us. I believe most of them had as much fun as we did. This book is dedicated to my parents, my current immediate family members, my brothers and sisters, aunts and uncles, cousins, grandparents, and the whole extended Italian clan that helped make growing up in the fifties. My thanks to Carolina DePaoli for her hard work restoring many of the photographs.

The final result was that most of us became good wise guys.

I hope you enjoy my stories. Maybe they will stir up your own "growing up" memories.

My Mom and Dad

My Dad

My dad, H. Martin DePaoli was one of the most mechanically gifted men I ever knew. I do not remember him ever not being able to fix something that was broken. He was the valedictorian of his high school class and graduated in 1932. However, he couldn't attend the ceremony because his family couldn't afford to get him a suit, and a suit was required. I believe that him not getting a college degree in engineering drove him to continually educate himself and to make sure that all of his children not only got a college education but also were taught to value education. Not being a good student was not an option in our household. Bad grades meant immediate lost privileges.

There were no jobs in 1932, and the first employment Dad ever had was as a farmhand on his uncle's farm. He worked for food. He got tired of menial work or no work at all and joined the navy. It was extremely competitive, but he was accepted. With unemployment rates at 25 percent or higher, everyone was trying to get into the navy. He spent four years in the navy and learned machinist skills. He thought about reenlisting but hated the cold weather and the North Atlantic where he had duty escorting Lend-Lease destroyers to England. He had a normal stature but was a muscular man, and in the navy, when ships used to have sports competition, he was an all-navy wrestler. He put in for a transfer to a ship in the Pacific fleet stationed in warm Pearl Harbor. He had met my mother by then, and she had vetoed reenlistment. He got out just before the Nazis invaded Poland. After that, no one got out of the service. Dad got a job making diesel aircraft engines and continued his education in mechanical skills. We all know what happened to the Pacific fleet at Pearl Harbor on December 7, 1941.

When the Japanese bombed Pearl Harbor, Dad wanted to enlist right away, but my mother, Anne, was nervous about him leaving for war. Finally, she relented, and he went back into the navy. He spent the duration of the war in the Pacific Theater participating in many naval battles. He spent a total of eight years serving his country. He had a broad understanding of the world and other people. In the navy he had traveled to many countries. He devoured newspapers and history books. Dad had incredible visual depth perception, which is very difficult to describe to people. He could visualize parts or items in three dimensions. Later in his working life, when company engineers designed a new part, they ran it by my father first for his opinion. He often told them what to adjust or correct so that the part would fit. The engineers who put aside their pride and listened to him made good parts. Those who didn't came back to him, and he performed the necessary adjustments on the part for them, never once saying I told you so.

Two weeks before the Japanese surrendered, he was accepted to Naval Aviation Schools Command. It was his dream fulfilled. He wanted to go, but because the war soon ended, the school dropped all quotas to zero.

Dad was creative and inventive. He held hundreds of patents for his company. In those days companies insisted that employees sign over anything they invented directly to the company. My dad never really complained about this. He remembered the Great Depression and did his best to keep the company in business.

He was well respected by his fellow skilled tradesmen and was president of the skilled trades union. Many people appreciated his reputation for being a fair man. My father was a man of his word. If he promised anyone anything, he made sure it happened. He has never lied to me, ever, not even a white lie to soothe my feelings or prevent my being afraid.

Dad also helped my aunts and uncles when they had car trouble. They would bring their cars over to our driveway, and by listening to the car, he could accurately tell them what was wrong. He also gave them a good idea of how much it would cost to fix it. Armed with this data, they could prevent local mechanics from taking advantage of them.

One particular story illustrates his character. When he was ninety years old, dad, my brother, and I sat in the same pew together in church. It was extremely hot, and the noisy fans did little to relieve the heat. The Mass was so full that people crowded in the side aisles because all the seats were taken. An obviously pregnant lady stood in the aisle near our pew. One of us got up and offered her his seat. If you guessed it was me or my brother, you're wrong. It was Pop.

First Holy Communion Picture with Mom and Dad

My Mom

My mom, Anne DiGuiseppe, was a hard-working and beautiful woman. She was the oldest of six children. She was an expert seamstress and great cook. She often made us homemade spaghetti, which was just terrific. The spaghetti sauce was perfect—not too spicy—and her meatballs would literally melt in your mouth. In our house something was always cooking or about to be cooked. All the tomatoes were homegrown in our garden. Her other specialties included stuffed peppers and lasagna. She was devoted to us all and often slept only four or five hours a night. She always seemed to have nonstop energy.

She had a good method of making homemade spaghetti and I assisted in the process. We used a large table and the spaghetti machine was in the middle. Once she had made the dough she would take a roller pin and flatten the dough out into similar rectangular shapes. Soon the first half of the table was filled up with flattened dough and the spaghetti cutting would begin. She would take the dough and slowly feed it through the spaghetti cutting machine. The shape perfectly fit the dimensions of the machine. There was no waste. I was in charge of slowly turning the crank on the machine. Mom would then collect the cut spaghetti that came out on the other side on the machine. She would place it in neat rows on the other half of the table. Amazingly she knew how to keep it from tangling and laid it out flat on the other half of the table in perfect symmetry.

Many of my cousins remember that when Mom got a hold of extra material or fabric, she made identical dresses for all of them. She knitted legendary colorful afghans and sweaters. She sent get well cards to members of the church when they were sick or in the hospital. She ran the spaghetti supper at the church for years. She canned much of our food that she raised in our home garden.

She was not afraid of a verbal fight and often made sure that her views and opinions were well known. She ran a tight household, and we all had to chip in with chores. She let us play but not until we had finished our homework. She was always there for us and sacrificed much for the family. She was a lovable and caring person.

The year before I entered first grade, Mom drove my older brother to school every day, and I usually went along. The school commute was about a half hour each way in our 1953 green Chevy. During this time, I stood up in the front seat of the car. I didn't want to miss anything, and I was small enough, under the height of a fireplug in our yard, that I fit standing up. During the ride, Mom drilled me on spelling, arithmetic, catechism, and other subjects. She had done homework with my brother every night, so the material was fresh in her mind.

My older brother was the only one of my siblings around in the fifties. For some reason we almost never fought or quarreled, mostly because we did not want to get in trouble with Dad or suffer confinement to our rooms. My other two sisters and one younger brother did not arrive until the sixties. Fortunately for them I had helped wear out Mom and Dad, and they got away with more hijinks than I could ever dream of.

Me Versus the Fireplug's Height

When I arrived the next year in first grade, I quickly got bored. But this was not because I was genius; I already knew most of the material. Luckily, Sister Mary Agnes, my teacher, noticed this and talked to my mom. Mom briefed her on what she had already covered, and the nun just adjusted and gave me other things to do and try in class. My generous older brother gave me mumps, chicken pox, measles, and few other childhood diseases, and I missed many days of school. But I never fell behind because Mom insisted—sick or not— that I do my homework, and she had already covered the material once with me.

My dad's love for his wife was obvious. They had their disagreements and arguments, like any other married couple, but they always put their kids first. When she was in a nursing home for the last three years of her life, Dad visited her twice a day every day.

Mom was deathly afraid of lightening. When they first built our house, Mom and Dad had enough money for the front and back entrance doors but not for closet doors. Still, Mom would hide in the closet with me and my brother during thunderstorms, feverishly praying a rosary while we were in there.

She prayed every day when I was in Vietnam. When I arrived home at the train station, she hugged me so hard I thought that she was going to crack a couple of ribs. After that she would always ask me first what I wanted for breakfast or dinner, much to the chagrin of my brothers and sisters. She was a special person who would do anything to help her family.

My Mom

The Spaghetti Supper

My mother ran the church spaghetti supper every year. It was usually held in January in the church auditorium. Mom was a superb organizer and handled every aspect of the benefit; all the profits went to the Sacred Heart parish. In an afternoon more than one thousand people were served an all-you-can-eat spaghetti supper. The entire family had to chip in and help. We stuffed envelopes that were mailed to parishioners, suffered paper cuts, set up tables and chairs, helped move equipment into the kitchen, and waited on tables. She ran this event for over twenty years.

She was adept at getting people to volunteer. Almost everyone in town knew my mother, and she was a hard woman to turn down when she asked you for help. She was a take-charge head of the supper and always pitched in when a crisis arose. I really think she enjoyed the social aspects of the whole event. She was an expert negotiator with suppliers and always got the lowest price or persuaded them to donate the items.

The spaghetti sauce, prepared by many old-world Italian ladies, was always superb. They made it the day before the supper and let it simmer until dinnertime. There were hundreds of gallons of sauce and thousands of meatballs ready to be served. People said the smell alone would draw diners in to the supper. Attendees were dressed in their Sunday best clothes and the auditorium was spotless. Large linen napkins were provided to all. Many of the patrons just tied them around their necks like bibs to prevent the sauce from splashing on their good clothes. There was no limit on the amount of spaghetti you could eat so many were soon loosening their belt buckles a notch or two. Mom worked hard on this event and kept accurate records for each year, which greatly helped in the planning of the next supper. When she finally "retired," another of my relatives took over the event and marveled at my mom's files and organization.

My Dad and Uncle Pasquale DiGuiseppe (Pat)

My dad and Uncle Pat were close friends. Uncle Pat, my mom's oldest brother, came over just about every week, and they sat at the kitchen table and discussed many things. I was fortunate enough to sit with them and just listen. They were both practical men. Uncle Pat was a master sergeant in World War II and worked as an engineer. He looked somewhat like Grandpa Liberatore. He was lanky and strong. I learned more from their discussions than from any university or school that I ever attended. They always consulted with each other on upcoming projects, home repairs, cars, politics, and a host of other topics.

Uncle Pat advised my dad to go for benefits first in negotiations with the company and not focus solely on pay increases. It paid off. My dad collected his pension for longer than he worked at the company, along with a great health care package.

I always looked forward to his visit. Uncle Pat asked what I was up to and respected my opinions on matters. Much later in life, he finally revealed to me that my PhD was useful for something. We were in the midst of a major snowstorm that had dumped about forty-eight inches on my dad's house. I was home at the time, and Dad and I went out after the first foot of snow. I had to shovel a path to a shed in the backyard to get the snow blower and shovels. Dad ran the snow blower, and I used the shovel. After an hour, we went inside while the snow continued to fall. Another foot of snow accumulated, so Dad and I went out again. Unfortunately, the snow blower needed gasoline, which was in the shed in the backyard. So I had to shovel the path to the backyard shed again to get the gas can. But this time, I put the gas can in the garage. We went out twice more to shovel a foot of snow each time. When Uncle Pat heard my tale of the gas can, he laughed and said, "Tommy, I knew that PhD. would come in handy for something!" To which I replied, "Yeah, I was beginning to wonder about that myself."

Both my dad and Uncle Pat were very proud of my making rank of captain in the Navy Reserve. Neither of them was much for praise or flattery, but when they heard that I had made that rank— both of them who were veterans of World War II—they remarked, "Tommy, that's pretty damn good!" Coming from them, this was high praise indeed.

Captain Tom   *PO1 Dad*

The Sad, Dark Day I Learned That Homework Might Be Forever

Forgetting homework or not getting it done was not an option. Mom checked and called one of my aunts or uncles to verify if I had no homework. I always had cousins and neighbors who were in the same grade with me. Unfortunately for me and because of this, I could not even try to lie about anything that I had been reprimanded for in school, because of too many "hostile" cousin witnesses. She got upset if she thought we were not getting enough homework, and she let my teachers know about it.

My family had a routine for doing homework—a well-oiled and disciplined approach— every school night. Once we finished supper, we cleared the table and did the dishes. We then brought our schoolbooks to the table and started our homework. My mother supervised, making sure we completed it. Once we were done, we had to help a brother or sister complete his or her work, like asking spelling words or catechism questions. Once we were *all* done, we could go outside and play until called into the house later. But if a brother or sister had trouble getting or understanding something, you helped or you wouldn't get a chance to play, no exceptions.

One Saturday when I was about ten years old, I saw my father sitting with two people, a woman and an African-American man, from his workplace. They were pouring over open books, doing math problems as he explained some things to them. The two adults were apprentices who wanted to become journeyman tool and die makers. But I didn't know this at the time. My mother was busy doing housework, but that didn't stop me from asking her what those two people were doing at the kitchen table with Dad. Not having the time to explain the full circumstances, she blurted out, "They are doing homework, Tommy." She then left the room to do other household chores. My heart dropped. I was devastated. Here sat "big people," and they were still doing homework! I had held out hopes that once you became an adult, the days of homework were gone. My dreams of eventual homework freedom were cruelly dashed.

Later on my dad explained to me that the people at our table that day were the apprentices who were to become journeymen in his company. He had taken on their training to ensure they received a fair shake. My father was the president of a skilled trades union. The automobile parts company wanted federal contracts that required minority hiring. Opposition was strong against such a move, but my dad, who was well respected by his fellow journeymen, appealed to their practicality and sense of job security. Because many of them had lived through the Great Depression and layoffs, he just reminded them that having government contracts would lessen the prospects of layoffs and increase the prospects of overtime. The new trainees were approved, and, because no one else volunteered to train them, Dad did.

An Army of Italian Aunts and Uncles

Being Raised by an Army of Italian Aunts and Uncles: Fall in or No Liberty or Privileges

Both of my parents came from large families. My dad had fifteen brothers and sisters; my mother had six. Almost all of them lived nearby in the same town where I was raised: Royersford, Pennsylvania. My aunts and uncles loved kids but were not afraid to correct or encourage me and my two brothers and two sisters. They also made sure my dad heard about any hijinks on my part, which made it extremely difficult to get away with any mischief, but that didn't stop me from trying. We also had a huge reunion every year that can only best be described as an orchestrated circus, beyond three rings, with fun and games for everyone. Birch beer and kids games kept us all entertained. My aunts and uncles ran all the kids games and made sure everyone at least got some prizes. The men played poker, and the women talked out their latest projects or hobbies.

My aunts and uncles were intensely loyal to each other. They had their animated arguments but never held grudges. My father was a tool and die maker who worked during the golden age of automobiles. He was mechanically gifted and read blueprints very well. Dad designed and built our boyhood home with help from his brothers. He then returned the favor by helping them build their houses.

My aunts were confident and competent women, boisterous with strong opinions on many issues. Most of all, they were positive with their children and their many nephews and nieces. They were quick to praise and encourage us, especially when we did something good. I was always amazed how they defended us all, even when we misbehaved. This reinforcement was a blessing for us. And the only way to describe their cooking skills is "world-class." Their meals were delicious and huge.

Most of my uncles were strong blue-collar men who worked hard and took care of their families. All of them served in World War II and had a great appreciation for this country and its principles. They were uncommonly practical and followed one of my dad's famous sayings: "If you can do something yourself, don't pay someone else to do it for you."

When we visited their homes, hospitality was the rule. My relatives offered my father and mother alcoholic drinks, and they took any refusal as an offense. They served children soda or Kool-Aid and cookies or other treats. My uncles often brought out a bottle of whiskey and poured a shot for the visitors, which they gulped down with varying facial expressions and winces.

One of the most admirable traits of my aunts and uncles was their ability to listen. They actually took the time to hear us kids and, mostly, answer our questions. They paid attention; they didn't ignore us. They also actually played games with me and my cousins. I know they truly believed that children were our future.

They also expected us to work hard, do chores, and to study in school. Their attitude toward our teachers (nuns) was that they were always right and you were always wrong. If you received a bad report or note from school, you could expect to be disciplined again when you got home. There was no appeal or escaping the punishment. They strongly understood the value of education. My family only accepted As and Bs. Receiving anything below that was a surefire way to get restricted or punished, such as being confined to your room for a period. In the fifties the only things in your room were some books and maybe sports equipment. This was much closer to solitary confinement than the video entertainment palace that is the bedroom of many kids today. The threat of being confined to your room greatly encouraged good behavior.

Later, when I arrived home by train from my army tour of duty in Vietnam, nearly every one of my aunts and uncles greeted me at the station. It still makes me emotional even today. They understood sacrifice and lived good lives. Their living example taught me much more than their words did.

Return from Vietnam

Uncle Mario, the Standup Comic

Uncle Mario DiGuiseppe was my godfather. He was my mom's younger brother. He was a husky guy and people often joked that he looked like a Mafia godfather. I did nothing to discourage this rumor. He was one of the quickest witted persons I have ever known. He was lightning-quick with jokes and sayings that made everyone laugh. Most of them were spontaneous. His type of humor was gentle, and everyone loved to have him around because he could make a joke about anything. He always seemed to find humor and goodness in any situation. He was very intelligent, and his humor reflected it. The best part about visiting his house was just listening to his latest jokes and sayings.

He had seven children and was married to Anna Marie. She was a fabulous cook and made the best lemon meringue pie that I've ever eaten. Like my other aunts she never said anything to discourage a child. She would often laugh the loudest at Uncle Mario's jokes.

Mario had lots of stories to tell about World War II and was proud that he was a security guard for General Eisenhower.

I couldn't have had a better godfather or better example of how to live a good life.

Uncle Mario, My Godfather

Aunt Alberta (Bert), My Personal Lawyer

Aunt Alberta Hozyash (DiGuiseppe), or Aunt Bert, was one of the most positive persons I have ever met. She was my mom's younger sister. She found the silver lining in even the direst events. She loved kids and enjoyed it when kids were having fun.

I often got into trouble over my mischievous tricks at home or at school. My teacher (a nun) and my mom often reprimanded me for my misdeeds. I was an adventurous kid who liked to be active and have fun. On many days I was over-the-top rambunctious.

My mom and dad were strict, and for most of my misdeeds the punishment was swift and certain. My mom was a strong-willed woman who wouldn't back down from the punishment that I received. There was never any time off for good behavior or early parole.

Many times when we went to Aunt Bert's home, my mom discussed my latest misadventures and punishment. When my mom argued with a person, she usually won, except for one person, her sister Alberta.

Aunt Bert defended me with the skill of a Clarence Darrow. The arguments she threw at my mom were astounding and convincing, maintaining that what I did was not so bad at all but normal, in fact, good. She had a strong and powerful voice. She was a gifted debater who often compared what I did to what her kids had done, and, of course, what I had done was not even worthy of a misdemeanor. In fact, many times Aunt Bert argued that instead of being punished I should be rewarded! I recall times when she persuaded my mom to not only rescind my punishment of being confined to my room but also to reward me with an ice cream cone or some other treat. She was one of the few persons who not only could hold her own with my mom but also could win an argument. She was married to my Uncle Joe who took me to Phillies games occasionally and shared his love of baseball with me.

I've often thought that she would have made a great defense attorney. She was my personal legal dream team. I know her positive attitude and praise of all my cousins had a good impact on them and their lives. I loved her a lot, and not just for eliminating many of my punishment days of confinement to my room.

Working for Uncle Ollie DiGuiseppe

One of the best persons I ever worked for was my Uncle Ollie. He wasn't really my uncle, just a cousin. When I was about eleven years old, he asked my mom and dad if I could come to work for him. He knew my family worked hard and wanted me to help him. He did various janitorial and lawn jobs for people. He paid his helpers cash and treated them well. He made sure we had lunch at a local bar. We usually ate a cheese steak or zep (sub sandwich) and a large soda. This was more fun than working.

Uncle Ollie was one of the hardest workers I ever met. He was also strong and powerful. He just loved to work and held many jobs at once. He also had a good sense of humor and enjoyed cigars. He pushed a leaf sweeper faster than anyone I ever saw. He was also polite and always called and asked my parents first if I could work for a few hours. He basically liked me because I worked and was not lazy.

He was not afraid to give you responsibility. I often ran the lawn tractors and loaded them onto the truck. He even let me drive the truck at the local dump for short distances. This is how I learned to drive a stick shift. He had a bunch of us working for him, but he soon realized I had a knack for janitorial work and always asked me to do the important jobs. The church auditorium was large and we would often scrub and wax it. First we would wet a large area with the floor with floor cleaner and Uncle Ollie would run the buffer with a brillo pad under it back and forth across the floor. We would then squeegee and clean up the dirty water. Next we would mop on two or three layers of wax on the floor and wait for it to dry. Then Uncle Ollie would put a buffing pad on the buffer and shine the floor to a gleam. Parishioners would often remark how clean and shiny the floor was. One of the most dangerous but fun jobs that we did was changing light bulbs in the church ceiling. The ceiling over the sanctuary was at least forty feet high and you had to climb up into the church attic. It was crossed with steel beams. The lights were close to or in the steel beams. You have to carefully walk on the steel beams, reach over and change the burnt out bulbs. If you fell off the beams or stepped on the unsupported ceiling drywall the danger was that you would fall through the drywall and drop forty feet to the sanctuary's marble floor.

When I was a senior in high school, I actually had a job as a janitor of a school where I put the lessons I learned from Uncle Ollie to good use. I loved janitorial work because you didn't have a boss constantly looking over your shoulder, and if you got all the tasks done, you kept out of trouble.

Mom laid out the rules for my pay from Uncle Ollie. I could keep 20 percent; the rest went into my savings account for college. No exceptions were allowed.

Uncle Ollie taught me that it's possible to have fun working and to enjoy it. I still rate being a janitor as one of the best jobs I've ever had.

Grandma and Grandpa

Bingo at Grandma's House

My grandma's, my mom's mother's house, was neat and spotless. She professionally arranged every object, every knickknack, atop a hand-knitted doily. There were religious objects and icons everywhere. She went to spectacular lengths to spoil us all with her wonderful cooking; her Italian cookies, such as pizzelles; and her ever-present Rolling Rocks orange soda.

The house always smelled like spaghetti sauce because there was always a pot of spaghetti sauce simmering on the stove with meatballs in it. You could take two slices of thick Italian bread, dip them into sauce, add meatballs, and have a delicious sandwich to eat. There was always olive oil around if you wanted to just eat the bread.

She often gave a history lessons to us grandkids when we were in her house. She had excellent knowledge about the history of our country and was extremely proud of it. Because my first name is Thomas, she had nicknamed me "Thomas Jefferson," with the emphasis on the *son*. With her strong Italian accent, she pronounced it *Thomas JefferSON*.

Grandma had a cuckoo clock that just fascinated us all. The bird would emerge every fifteen minutes and we would never tire of watching it and trying to predict how many cuckoos it would cuckoo.

We begged our parents to let us go on "vacation" to Grandma's house for a week. No one misbehaved or acted out at Grandma's. None of my cousins ever fought with me since I was the second oldest grandson and bigger than all of them. That week was paradise with superb food, great stories, sleeping late, and nonstop games of bingo.

My grandma was a world-class bingo player. She loved to play the game. Her sons and daughters drove her to local bingo places, churches, wherever a game was on. She had a well-earned reputation, and her house was filled with prizes that she often gave away as gifts. One entire second-story bedroom was filled with her winnings. She would play for hours on end or until the bingo establishments closed.

Grandma was always neatly dressed in a dress and clean. No dirt existed very long in her house. She would quickly get household chores done and had a well-organized method of cleaning up dishes. As soon as something was out of order it was immediately corrected. She never wasted anything and leftovers often reemerged in soup or side dishes.

Grandma organized the grandkids' bingo games. We all sat around the kitchen table, each of us grandkids watching one or two bingo cards with buttons in hand to place on the cards. The cards were wrinkled with tuned up corners but readable. The stakes were high to us. Each bingo game winner received a penny! We thought that was exorbitant. You could then pile up your winnings next to where you played. Orange sodas sat around the table in various stages of being emptied. Our frequent burps accentuated the bingo number calling.

I was amazed at Grandma's bingo skills. She could watch a dozen or more bingo cards of her own. At the same time, she could look at or audit your cards and help you out if you missed a number. She never rebuked you if you missed a number but just smiled, sort of winked, and put a button on the missed number. You could tell she relished playing bingo. The best part was we also enjoyed it, and we never tired of playing with Grandma.

Grandpop and Grandmom

Getting to Light Grandpa's Pipe

My grandpa was named Liberatore DiGuiseppe. His nickname was Jake. He worked for almost forty years on the railroad as a laborer. In those days small groups of men were given full responsibility for the complete maintenance of about fifty miles of track. Transportation was not provided to the work site. The crew walked to work every day. Grandpa didn't have a car and had to travel about ten miles by foot just to get to the start of his track area. He walked faster than most people jogged. He was a tall man, wiry, and his strides were long and sure. He had a terrific shock of thick hair. He loved outside work, which was fortunate, and there were no rain days or snow days off.

His appetite was legendary. He could eat a whole pound of spaghetti in one sitting. He ate spaghetti when it was cold. The routine at dinner was that everyone took the amount of spaghetti they wanted out of the bowl first. The rest went to Grandpa. His breakfast consisted of Italian bread with an oil dressing and salt on top, with a cup of strong coffee. He meticulously packed six or seven sandwiches for his lunch. Each had one slice of bologna, and he trimmed any meat that hung over the bread and used it for another sandwich.

He was an early riser and never used an alarm clock, but he was never late for anything. Often he worked his garden in the very early morning before walking to work. He hand-dug his garden every year.

He had a railroad pass, and he and his family could travel the railroads. He took them to Canada and to other states in the U.S. He worked in Washington, D.C., for a while when the railroad transferred him there, and he would return home on weekends. He was proud to be an American and took a family picture at the Capitol. He often went to South Philadelphia to purchase salami and other meats for the family. He would trace an outline of his children's feet and purchase shoes there.

My uncles testified that he had the strongest grip of any man they ever knew. He was always the one called upon to turn a pipe wrench or to loosen up some rusted bolt on equipment. His disposition was pleasant, and he often told jokes to people at which he laughed the loudest at himself.

One tale, which comes from an uncle and has been hard for me to verify, relates an incident at a local bar where a man sucker punched Grandpa while he was at the bar. My uncle says Grandpa didn't even flinch or move when the man hit him. Grandpa grabbed the man's upper arms, squeezing them in an iron grip, and lifted him straight up above his head so the man was kicking in pain as he was lifted. All Grandpa said to the man was, "Don't do that again." He placed the man square back down on his feet, and the assailant rolled around the floor trying to relieve the pain in his arms. The entire bar had witnessed the incident, and my uncle said dead silence and awe prevailed. A number of men tried to attend to the man who had punched my Grandpa. Luckily, the he had no broken bones, but my uncle said he had broken blood vessels in his upper arms from Grandpa's grip. Grandpa never had any trouble again at the bar.

My uncle also mentioned that Grandpa never had any trouble with his sons, who understood not to cross him. But he had a sense of mischievousness also, which his sons loved. In many ways he was a big kid having fun in life.

He was also good with math. He could add, subtract, multiply, and divide numbers faster than most calculators. I heard a story that when he went through the checkout counter at the local grocery store, he would tell the clerk exactly to the penny what he owed. At first the clerks checked the totals on the old-fashioned machines or by hand. Soon they realized he was always right, and his reputation for honesty in town was well known. The routine soon became, "Liberatore (or Jake), what do you owe us today?" "One dollar and nineteen cents, and here it is." Many times they helped him pack the groceries immediately as he approached the counter— before he paid.

I think he had memorized a lot of passages from the Bible. He once worked in a store that sold religious articles. He could quote from scripture and could tell Bible stores with more color and vigor than they were written in the actual text. He also had a great deal of faith in his Catholic church. He knew the particular saint for almost every day of the year and could tell you what each saint was the patron of. I never heard him swear or curse at anyone. He had a great sense of faith. He loved America and was very grateful for this country and for freedom. All of his sons served in the armed forces.

He always wanted to be first in many things. When a new technology or invention came out, he had to be the first to have it or try it. He had the first telephone on his block and the first TV. One of the best stories of all is about my Aunt Lucy, or Lucia, as he called her. Grandpa wanted her to be musical and enjoy music. The day after she was born, he went out and bought a new piano for her. This was at the height of the Depression, and money was extremely tight. Grandma was worried, but they struggled and made the monthly payments for the piano. Eventually, my Aunt Lucy went on to play the organ in our church for over forty years, and so did her daughters. Aunt Lucy was my godmother and was a lot like my own mother. She treated all of us like honored guests when we were in her house, and she had a great sense of humor. She always encouraged me and could argue well with anyone. She spoke her opinion and was not intimidated by anyone One of my classmates called her a "knockout" once, and not understanding what it meant, I was ready to come to blows with him. He was right, however; she was a beautiful knockout. Her nickname for me was Tom Tom the Piper's son, for no apparent reason. Everything I did, no matter if it was good or bad, was just "wonderful" to her.

Grandpa had a large, old-fashioned pipe. He stuffed tobacco in it and lit it with a big match with a self-igniting tip. Once lit, the smell of tobacco permeated the entire house. But he didn't smoke it very often, so the smell of smoke didn't linger in the house. If he had heard that you had been an especially good boy or girl, he would give you the match, let you strike it, and have you give the lit match back so that he could light the tobacco in the pipe. Whoever did this was thrilled, especially enjoyed the smell of the tobacco, and was very proud that Grandpa had trusted him or her to help. Of course, after he took a few puffs from the pipe, he made you listen to his jokes, which I think he often tried out on us as an experimental audience. Most of them were very funny.

He was a good, strong, kind man who we all loved.

Parochial School Tales

The Art of Baseball Card Flipping

TOPPS baseball cards cost a nickel and were highly valued. The cards in each packet were assigned randomly. When you purchased a packet of cards, you had no way of knowing if the baseball players you got were any good or if the cards were valuable. The flat bubble gum included was mostly for decoration and was stiff and tasteless. Somehow the scent of the bubble gum transferred to the cards but eventually wore off. There was a lot of negotiating and trading of the cards with your buddies. The better players usually demanded multiple cards just as in real major league baseball player trades.

One of the games we played with the cards was flipping. We picked out a wall, and each player would flip one of his cards against the wall. Often the cards' corners would get bent. It was sort of a baseball card version of craps or dice throwing. The object of the game was to get your card closer to the wall than the other players' cards. It was a winner-takes-all game. Most players never risked a good player in the game of flip. Players had to adjust for weather conditions, including wind, to get their card closest to the wall. The farther away from the wall, the more the element of luck was involved. Arguments usually resulted in the declaration of a tie and a reflip. On occasion arguments got heated.

One day at recess, I was playing a game of flip with Jim. I thought I had clearly won Jim's baseball card, but he objected by punching me in the mouth. I retaliated with a blow to his eye. The results were a cut lip and a black eye. Almost instantaneously Sister Michael Jerome swooped down upon us. To us she was a giant, over six feet tall and very athletic. She could hit a baseball three times farther than any of us could. She grabbed Jim and me both by the scruff of our necks, unceremoniously dragged us back to our classroom, and instructed us to sit in our desks until recess was over. She ominously promised that she would "deal" with us shortly. We were in big trouble.

When recess was over, the rest of the class returned to the classroom and quietly settled into their desks. Sister Michael Jerome announced that fighting during recess would never be tolerated. Unfortunately for Jim and me, a graphic demonstration was about to take place. Not content to have an audience of just one class, Sister Michael Jerome led two other classes into the back of the classroom to watch. The drama began to grow, and the only thing I could think of was from the Passion Week gospel and the scene about the prisoner Barabbas. I was hoping my classmates would shout, "Give us Tom! Release Tom!" to Sister Michael Jerome. This didn't happen. Instead, Sister ordered Jim and me to stand and go to the front of the classroom. There was dead silence in the classroom. No one moved or uttered a peep. I remember the wind blowing into the open classroom windows and rustling the test papers that hung around the room. Sister grabbed a thick ruler and told us to stick our arms out with palms down. Jim and I knew what was coming and were smart enough to not pull our hands back as Sister Michael Jerome delivered ten hard blows across our knuckles. The pain was severe, but neither one of us cried or yelled out. I saw my schoolmates closing their eyes and wincing. The punishment had been swift and certain. We were allowed to immediately return to our seats, and Sister led the other classes out and back to their classrooms. Later in the afternoon, Sister showed some mercy. She told Jim and me to report to the nurse's office where the school nurse put bags of ice on our knuckles.

Needless to say, for the rest of the year no fighting occurred during recess. The two pugilists had been appropriately punished, and during the next recess, I even shook hands with Jim and we continued flipping baseball cards. Jim and I reconciled and agreed not to argue about baseball cards anymore.

In a stroke of playground genius, we agreed to have an appointed umpire, Donna Lombardi, settle our disputes. We continued to enjoy many games of baseball card flipping during recess. I knew Donna loved Tastykake treats, so whenever I had an extra one, I "shared" it with her. For some reason many of the close calls in baseball card flipping, delivered by umpire Donna, went in my favor. Ironically, Donna eventually married Jim, but I don't think she has ever mentioned my Tastykake strategy to him.

So I won the fight (well maybe a draw), experienced swift and painful punishment from Sister Michael Jerome, had the satisfaction of not crying or complaining about the punishment, but eventually lost the girl (newly appointed baseball card flipping umpire Donna Lombardi) to Jim. They can't make B movies with plots any better than this incident.

When I got home, I expected my dad to discipline me, but he asked what happened to the other guy. I said, "I gave him a black eye." He smiled and said, "Good, but don't let it happen again."

My Altar Boy Career

I was required to be an altar boy for our church. I didn't really want to be one, but it was expected of me. The nuns at my school trained the altar boys. They also showed somewhat blatant favoritism for altar boys, holding out faint hope that we would get a vocation and become priests. With my tendency to commit classroom mischief, I needed all the favoritism I could get. We had to learn Latin, and all the responses to the replies were in Latin. We were issued surplices and cassocks. My mom spent hours cleaning and ironing my surplice and cassock to make sure that I looked presentable at Mass. I was actually an altar boy in the procession when the bishop dedicated our Sacred Heart Church in 1955.

Masses in those days were quick; some priests could complete a Mass in thirty-five minutes. One of the tough tasks that I had was being the server for Mass during Lent. The service started at 6 a.m., and I had to serve every day during Lent. I remember doing a lot of yawning and struggling not to tip over during the service.

After Mass, I went down to the dark and dingy school auditorium and ate breakfast. It sort of smelled like sour milk and leftovers. I had a Tupperware enclosure filled with Kellogg's Frosted Flakes and a spoon. I loved Frosted Flakes not only because they tasted good but also because there were free plastic, green army men in the box. I had at least a platoon of such men, and their ranks were growing. To complete my breakfast, I purchased a carton of milk at five cents from the milk vending machine, filled up the container, and ate. Cold cereal on cold mornings was not the most enjoyable combination for breakfast. When I had an extra dime, I went to the Coke vending machine, bought a bottle of Coke, and drank it down. The church and school always kept the heat down to save money, so the whole experience still chills my bones today.

I don't know why, but my breakfast of champions—Frosted Flakes, milk, and Coca-Cola—has not caught on yet with sports nutritionists.

My altar boy career progressed every year, and I received more responsibilities. In my final year, I reached the highest honor an altar boy can receive: I was named master of ceremonies for the midnight Easter Mass. This was one of the most complicated services, and I had to know my duties as well as the duties of every other altar boy. Everything went without a hitch. I retired at the top. I still remember most of the Latin.

The Altar boy

Our Home Traditions

Our Garden

We always had a large garden in our backyard. Garden is a misnomer; it was more like a small truck farm. Our yard had some of the richest soil in the nation and had formerly been an apple orchard. We grew all sorts of vegetables and fruits: corn, tomatoes, cucumbers, watermelon, and cantaloupes. One item we were not short of was hoes. Dad assigned us the daily task of weeding the garden and tilling up the soil with hoes. Dad also used his mechanical precision to organize the garden. The rows of vegetables and corn were perfectly straight and no space was wasted. He had a system of crop and row rotation than changed every year. Almost everything grew, including weeds. We had to make sure that we chopped down the weeds and not the vegetables. Dad checked our work when we were done, and we incurred his criticism if we cut down any vegetables by mistake. I soon developed calluses on the inside of my hands from working in the garden every day. We usually did this in the morning because it was cooler and because more pressing things, like the neighborhood baseball game, were later.

During drought years, we hauled buckets of water and used sprinkler cans to water the plants. I soon developed an appreciation for good growing weather and rain.

When my dad and uncles built the house, they installed a cesspool in the back section of the garden. The crops always grew faster and better over this area. That garden provided much of our family food. My mother spent many hours canning the vegetables and the tomatoes. Mom used those tomatoes in spaghetti sauce, which were a kitchen staple and our most frequent meal.

Pancakes on Friday

As Roman Catholics we didn't eat meat on Fridays. We did, however, enjoy what we all thought was a treat for Friday supper: pancakes. We all gathered around to watch my dad create the batter and slowly pour the pancakes onto a hotplate. Dad was exceptionally precise in his pancake making. Without fail, he created perfect round pancakes of the exact size. I still do not know how he did it. There were no bigger or smaller pancakes. This prevented fights over who would get the bigger pancake. When we sometimes had guests, they also were mesmerized by the precision of the pancake assembly line.

We all watched attentively as Dad carefully poured the batter onto the hotplate. The pancakes crackled, quickly cooked, and turned light brown. Dad quickly lifted up the cooked ones with a spatula and put them on a big serving plate. The rules were you had to wait until Dad put the serving plate on the table before you could grab the number of pancakes you wanted. The first three or four serving plates disappeared in minutes. Dad rotated two or three serving plates and stopped only after he asked everyone if they wanted any more pancakes.

Of course, having access to syrup, jelly, and other sugary toppings for the pancakes added to the enjoyment. Even into our college years, my brothers and sisters and I continued to enjoy the tradition of pancake Fridays. The mystery of Dad's technique for precise perfectly round pancakes, however, remains unsolved.

Christmas Gifts

Christmas at our house was a big and exciting event. My mother decorated the house beautifully. The Christmas tree was always a natural pine decorated with lights and tinsel. It stood in the corner of the living room with a wire tied to it so it wouldn't fall down. My little sister had once managed to pull down the entire tree upon herself. My parents hung blue lights around the door on the outside of the house and placed electric candles in the sill of each window.

Each of us kids asked for one big gift each year. My brother and I asked for two-wheel bikes one year. On Christmas morning, we leapt from our beds, rushed downstairs, and looked around. But no bikes. Mom and Dad saw our disappointment, chuckled, and told us we should look around the house. We found the two new bikes on the back porch. Dad, as usual, had put them together perfectly.

The first time I took my new bike to school; I fell off and tore a big hole in the knee of my pants. Mom and Dad didn't yell at me when I came home. My mother, who was an expert seamstress, just sewed up the hole and urged me to be more careful and watch the traffic.

Another time I asked for a five-cell flashlight so that I could use it to send Morse code messages to my friend across the street. We spent hours sending secret messages to each other. We provided a lot of business for battery manufacturers.

We always exchanged Christmas gifts at Grandma's house. Because the family was so large, every cousin's name was put into a hat, and my aunts and uncles pulled out names. The Christmas scene at Grandma's house was absolutely chaotic. My cousins ripped open presents and ran around the house with their new toys. Every cousin got one gift, but the name of the aunt or uncle was not put on the gift. It added to the excitement of Christmas and the family Christmas meal.

The Christmas meal was even more hectic with everyone talking about his or her gifts and constantly passing the delicious Italian food and orange soda. Because of the large number of guests, tables were not only in the kitchen and dining room, but also in the living room. There were separate kids' tables where all of us marveled about how good Santa had been to us, despite being somewhat naughty. We never fought or teased each other. Our aunts and uncles would have never allowed it to happen.

My Christmas Story

My Paper Route Ordeal: "It will be a good experience for you, Son."

When I was about ten years old, Dad volunteered me to have a paper route in town. His comment was, "It will be a good experience for you, Son." Our local paper was published weekly, on Thursday evenings. I had to deliver more than a hundred newspapers over about a two-mile area in town. I also had at least ten churches along my route. The pay was $1.27 per week. I received my money in a small brown envelope when the papers were dropped off at a local funeral home porch. I rolled up the newspaper and put a rubber band around them. The rubber bands I had to pay for myself. Then I had to stuff the papers into two canvas newspaper carrier bags, blazoned with the name of the newspaper, which I crisscrossed over my shoulders. With all that weight, I moved just a shade faster than a turtle.

There was no list for me of who was to receive the papers along my route. I guess relational databases had not been invented yet. The first week, the man who delivered or dropped off the papers walked the route with me. The former paperboy had quit. I should have known that was a bad omen. It was expected I would remember the hundred or so houses (and churches) that received the newspapers from this one-time crash course.

Most of the houses were made of brick, at least three stories and huge. The lawns were well kept, but some had more weeds than grass. Huge trees grew along the street and in people's front yards, which caused many of my newspaper throws to ricochet off target. Traffic on many of the streets was light or nonexistent.

In the winter I delivered the last half of the route in the dark, but the streetlights provided at least some illumination for me. Despite the one-week crash course, my solo run on week two wasn't a total disaster, and surprisingly only two people complained that they didn't get the paper. There was not much customer turnover or additions to the route. The newspaper consisted mostly of local news and advertisements. I sometimes made the paper because of my Little League exploits. I believe it cost ten cents.

The first half of the route was a journey out of hell, up steep hills with all the newspapers still weighing me down. It wasn't until I was half done and the load of newspapers lightened that I could pick up some speed.

Along the route, I received all sorts of detailed instructions from people who subscribed to the newspaper. They were friendly, but they made sure I understood they were special customers and deserved special treatment. Some wanted the paper between the screen door and the house door. Some wanted it in their mail box. Some wanted it on their porch. Most wanted it where it would minimize their personal steps to get to the paper. Most thought their requests were reasonable.

The first year, I did my best to meet all of these special requests. But I soon learned a hard lesson. Traditionally, a Christmas gift envelope for the newspaper boy was given to all customers. I was shocked when I collected these gifts to learn how cheap people were and how nasty they could be with their notes about my fulfilling or not fulfilling their special newspaper delivery requests.

My route technique soon underwent a radical change. I delivered the paper in the manner that took the least amount of time and effort on my part. Special requests be damned! Surprisingly, I didn't get much flak for this. When customers tried to approach me to make special delivery requests, I smiled politely and continued quickly on my route.

I also tried using a bike to help me deliver faster. Unfortunately, the route and stops were laid out in such a manner that a bike didn't help much. The newspapers also made the bike so front heavy that stability was a major issue. When it rained, delivery was just miserable, and I had to make sure the newspapers were covered from the rain. The company didn't provide plastic wraps or waxed paper for the newspapers, or perhaps they weren't invented yet.

I asked the newspaper company for a favor and quickly learned that many companies are not flexible when it comes to employee requests, especially from an employee who makes $1.27 a week. I asked the newspaper to deliver approximately fifty papers to the funeral home and make a second delivery of fifty papers to a local gas station about halfway along the route. The idea was to reduce the weight of the newspapers when I started out. This idea was rejected, and the deliveryman went out of his way to inform me that it was the stupidest idea he had ever heard of from any paperboy ever.

This response convinced me of my next step. As soon as I collected my Christmas gift envelopes the following year, I quit without notice. I gave the right excuse to my dad by telling him I wanted to spend more time studying for school. It was an obvious but pretty good white lie. I understand the deliveryman had to deliver the papers himself for four months before they hired another paperboy.

This episode taught me that I wouldn't make my fortune in the newspaper business. It also taught me that whenever my Dad said, "It will be a good experience for you, Son," I was in deep trouble.

Notre Dame Football and Perfect Spirals

There was only one football team in our household that we were allowed to listen to or root for: Notre Dame. We always listened to Notre Dame games on the radio or watched them when they came on TV. My dad was one of the most animated Notre Dame fans ever. He really got into the games, cheering and shouting advice all throughout. He lived and died with the success of Notre Dame football.

He had experienced discrimination as a Catholic and as an Italian in our town and had learned to overcome it. He often said, "They can discriminate against us Catholics, give us lousy jobs and make fun of us, but we can beat them in what really counts, football!"

He was fairly athletic himself and had played some semipro football as a quarterback after the war. He often jokingly remarked how quarterbacks are protected in today's game. He would say, "Why don't they put a skirt on them. When I played, they basically tried to knock the quarterback, me, out of the game."

When I attended Notre Dame, I took him to a game in South Bend when Notre Dame played Navy. We sat in the end zone, and people must have thought we were crazy because we cheered for both teams. As plays developed he would make remarks such as, "Number forty-one was holding." Sure enough, the referee would shortly announce over the microphone, "Holding. Offense, number forty-one." Once you've viewed the game as a quarterback, you have a different perspective than the average fan.

Thirty years later, to the day, when my daughter was attending Notre Dame, we all went to another Notre Dame versus Navy game. Dad hadn't lost his touch and called out penalties before the referees did. Luckily, Notre Dame won both games.

Dad often played catch with me with a football. The football was of the old-school style, designed more for kicking than for passing. I'd run receiver patterns, and he'd throw the pass to me. We would play for hours. What I remember most was that every pass was precise, a perfect spiral with no wobble. This was yet another skill Dad had mastered.

Pop One of Notre Dame's Greatest Fans (Courtesy Sylvia Kresock)

Baseball in the 1950s

Choosing Sides in Baseball

The first step in choosing sides in baseball is a tradition many people are familiar with. The two team captains both got a grip on the bottom of a baseball bat. Each would alternately move his hand up the bat, gripping it as he went until he reached the nub on the end of the bat. The last captain would get his best grip on the nub and then hold it away from his body at arm's length. The other captain got three kicks to try to knock the bat out of the other captain's grip. If he succeeded, he got the first pick. If the captain holding the bat held on, he got first pick. In our neighborhood it was a great honor to be picked first, but everyone was eventually picked.

Earl, the One-Crutch Baseball Player

Earl, one of our best neighborhood ballplayers, had a leg deformity and had to use a crutch to play baseball. He was so good that he was usually one of the first guys picked. He had figured out how to maneuver, run, hit, and field with one good leg and one crutch. He could actually outrun many guys with his hop-along technique. No one ever made fun of him or teased him. He loved to play and often played the outfield where he ran down pop flies, caught the ball, and threw it accurately back to the infield. Often he played center field and fielded balls that the right fielder or left fielder should have caught. And, yes, his baseball cap would often fly off when he ran after and caught a fly ball. He could accurately aim the ball when he was at the plate, holding the bat with one arm and usually hitting it where we were not playing him. He was difficult to tag out because he could put the crutch on the base instead of sliding, which was a neighborhood rule we allowed.

He had major skills at arguing close calls and often performed magnificent reenactments of the play showing exactly what happened, where the ball was, and how the runner was safe or out. His actions and expressions were operatic. His exaggerations were tremendous.

He was way ahead of his time with this orchestrated manual instant replay. He would have made a great major league manager, especially when arguing with the umpires.

Eventually, Earl outgrew the condition and no longer needed the crutch, which made him an even better ballplayer. He taught us all a lesson: you can overcome any so-called handicap and still be darn good at what you love.

One-Hundred-Eighty-Foot Solo Baseball

The home run fence in our local Little League Park was about 180 feet from home plate. I not only knew this distance to be accurate but had actually paced it off.

To sharpen my skills, I played a game of solo baseball in our backyard. I would throw the ball up in the air and try to hit it as hard as I could. I always used the newest baseball that I had; my theory was that it would fly higher or travel farther. I also used the best bat, the one with fewest cracks and screws in it, to maximize the distance. I had paced out various landmarks or trees in my yard and knew the distances from where I usually batted.

I spent many hours playing this game of solo baseball hoping to break the 180-foot barrier. Weather conditions didn't matter. I played in the rain and hot sun. It was often oppressively hot and humid during the summer, but I kept throwing the ball up in the air and swinging as hard as I could. I often heard the cicada's loud call while I was playing this solitary game of home run derby. Because I had only one good baseball, I retrieved the ball after each hit and then went back to "home plate" to hit the next one. There was a lot of walking in this game and lots of flub hits, but I don't really remember completely missing the ball very often when I threw it up in the air.

Imagination was a critical part of this game. I often put myself in situations like batting in the bottom of the ninth of the seventh game of the World Series. Major league pitchers were also on the mound bearing down on me. I kept whacking the ball, retrieving it, and then walking back to home plate. I never really got tired or bored with this game.

During my last year of Little League—I clearly remember it was a Friday—I finally hit the ball more than 180 feet and past the tree landmark in my backyard. I was elated and actually went into a home run trot when I retrieved the baseball. More importantly, I knew that I had the power and confidence to hit a home run in a game situation.

A week later I was playing for the Warriors, my Little League team. We wore green caps and wool uniforms. Wool was used in an attempt to make the uniforms indestructible so they could be passed down from year to year. But playing in wool made you hot. Luckily, the league provided us with plenty of water, which we drank out of a bucket (usually, but not always, devoid of dead bugs) in the dugout from a long-handled metal cup.

In the game, I hit a home run that barely cleared the left field fence. I didn't think I had hit the ball that hard, so I ran as hard as I could with my head down. It was not until I rounded second base that I heard the third base coach yell, "Slow down, Tommy. It went over the fence." I quickly went into a good home run trot, and all my teammates mobbed me when I crossed the plate. When they asked me if I had known it was going out, I sheepishly responded, "I thought I hit it good but wasn't sure, so I kept hustling."

One-hundred-eighty-foot solo baseball had finally paid off.

The Left-Handed Glove and How to Survive in Right Field

My favorite baseball glove was a left-hander's mitt. It fit my hand perfectly. There was absolutely no slack and I could control it. I liked it because it was broken in and closed as soon as a ball hit. Most of my catches were immediately trapped in the web of the glove. Because it hit the glove web almost instantly, the ball was away from my palm and did not sting at all. I, of course, kept it well-oiled and taken care of. My glove stayed in my bedroom when I wasn't on the ball field. It didn't have any player's signature on it, and the brand name had worn off. I can't remember any ball ever bouncing off of it or falling out once it closed.

Playing right field is a challenge for any ball player, especially a neighborhood ball player. It's just downright boring. The odds of a ball being hit to you are slim to none. The challenge is to keep yourself entertained but not completely out of the action. I would put my hands on my knees, hunch down, and rock back and forth on my heels and toes. I would stand up straight and do side body twists periodically. Pounding my fist into the glove incessantly was another tactic I used to stay engaged with the game. I would bend down and pick out a long weed, put it in my mouth, and chew on it. The heavy end of the weed would drop down below my mouth. Then I would spit it out and get a fresh weed. The area around my spot soon came devoid of weeds, so I moved over a couple of feet.

It was bright and brutal in right field. I always pulled my baseball cap down as far as I could to shade out the sun. I let my shirttail hang out and tucked it in when the half inning was over and we went in to bat. Trying to catch flies or other bugs right out of the air was another diversion. Saying some baseball banter was also periodically attempted. However, the voice of a bored right fielder often has an eerie sound like a man falling off a cliff. The few times that a ball was hit to right field, it was always best to run in on the ball so at least you looked as if you were paying attention. Playing right field prepared me well for waiting in long lines, boredom, and political speeches later in life. I owe a lot to my right field days.

In Right Field, Number 21, Tommy DePaoli!

More Reasons Why Baseball Was King in the Fifties

In our neighborhood almost all of the houses had good-sized lots where we could play baseball. The homes were modest but well kept. Baseball skills take a long time to learn, but just about everyone in our neighborhood mastered the basic knowhow of catching a pop fly and fielding a grounder. Many people can't understand how we played baseball for hours and hours in the 1950s. After all, baseball is labeled a boring game. We had a neighborhood team and played in a lot across the street from my house. Our parents could literally look out the window and see us playing. If we were lucky, we had enough equipment for everyone or at least a glove for everyone. We played all day long. We chose sides and got the games started. We stopped only for lunch, supper, or rain.

Our brand of baseball was not boring because of the way we modified the rules. There were no coaches, spectators, umpires, or adults to slow down the game. Each batter got three swings or strikes. There were no called balls or called strikes because there was no umpire. A batter had to swing at a pitch, so there was even less delay. Batters were not allowed to go through a routine in the batter's box. You got up to the plate, dug in, and got ready to swing. Often when we were in the field, we yelled out to our own pitcher to get the ball over the plate and let the batter hit it.

There was no stealing base, usually because someone from the other team played catcher when they were up. Time outs were not allowed. Disputes over whether a player was out or safe at a base were argued with the skill of a Philadelphia lawyer with much drama and terrific action. If both sides couldn't come to an agreement, a coin flip settled the call. Innings went by quickly, and so did the games.

Equipment was patchwork. Uniforms were our play clothes or dungarees. Our caps were from our Little League team. Most of the wooden bats had cracks in them and were held together by tar tape and wood screws. Just about everyone had a glove or mitt, but they were not premium models. Many of the balls came from the local Little League. Often foul balls hit in Little League flew into a farmer's weedy field, and players were sent to find them. Sometimes these players would hide the baseballs and come back later when no one was around and find the lost ball. Thus our supply of baseballs was usually ample thanks to this ploy.

There were definite boundaries for a home run. In our field, a home run was over the row of hedges in the outfield. A fielder could actually run through the hedges and catch a home run, but this didn't happen very often because it was a nasty, thorny hedge.

Sometimes on hot days, someone's mom would bring us a pitcher of Kool-Aid, which everyone slammed down quickly and then got back to playing as soon as possible. Games often lasted until it got dark.

This brand of quick modified baseball worked well for us. Perhaps the current baseball commissioner should consider some of our neighborhood rules to speed up the game.

The Neighborhood Guys

The Fallout Shelter

Nuclear weapons and the threat of nuclear war were a big part of the fifties. Schools held duck-and-cover drills. The news always covered the threat that the Soviet Union could start a nuclear war. Worse yet was Hollywood's fascination with radiation and all sorts of giant insects and other creatures spawned by nuclear testing and radiation.

We often went to watch these Hollywood B monster movies at the local theater. My favorite was *Them*, a movie about giant ants that attacked Los Angeles. The best way to kill them was to shoot them in the antennae. We spent Saturdays viewing movies like this when we could. These preposterous movies affected kids. TV didn't show much that interested us. For most of the guys, our favorite show was *Superman*, which came on at seven o'clock on Monday nights.

Some of my neighborhood pals and I decided one day to build a fallout shelter. There was a farmer's field behind a friend's house, and, like many fields, had a thin strip of windbreak trees surrounding it. We often played army in those woods and built tree houses.

Our plan was simple: dig a big hole and get underground in case of a nuclear war. We dug a big hole, about fifteen-by-fifteen feet and at least eight or nine feet deep. Unfortunately, we didn't account for water entering the hole or draining into the hole. We made some lame attempts to waterproof it and get the water out, but they all failed. We then decided that we would have to use the fallout shelters in town in case of nuclear attack. We filled the hole back up and continued to play army and build tree houses.

The Neighborhood Wise Guys

I grew up with a large neighborhood group of pals. We were all about the same age and played together daily. We played baseball, football, and basketball. We also played army and other games we made up. Bobby was one of my best pals. He was a tall, strong kid. He was very good at baseball, often robbing me of hits not only in our neighborhood games but also in Little League games. Russell excelled at football and ran well. Jack had an adventurous streak and was a flat-out daredevil.

We all had parents who were strict but cared about us. If they saw us doing something they didn't like, they came out and stopped it cold. We were all curious about the things we were not supposed to do. We tried cigarettes and cigars and got sick. We made explosives and rockets from ground-up match heads. Usually the explosions were weak. We occasionally brought out our plastic model airplanes, which we had assembled, and poured gasoline over them and watched them burn into unrecognizable globs of plastic.

Fistfights were infrequent, but we wouldn't let other kids from other neighborhoods harass any one of us.

Most of us grew up and turned out to be pretty good wise guys.

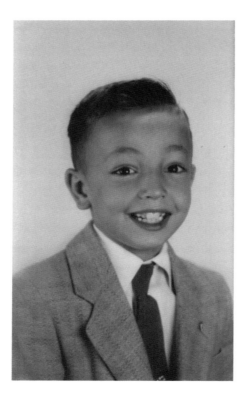

A Semi Good Wise Guy

Epilogue

In 1959 when the 50's came to a close I was twelve years old. I had just finished my best year ever in Little League and started the seventh grade. I now had more cousins and was soon to get more brothers and sisters. Our extended family remained close throughout the 60's and I received more advice, chores, love, and responsibility. Today whenever I have a tough decision to make in life I always ask myself, "What would mom and dad do?" I often look back on the guidance that my aunts and uncles gave me. They did their best to make sure I understood what was important in life. Integrity and family. I hope that I have not disappointed them.

Made in the USA
Charleston, SC
15 September 2013